Vision &
Strategy

DORIS ROTHAUER

Vision & Strategy

Strategic Thinking for Creative and Social Entrepreneurs

BIRKHÄUSER
Basel

Content

Dear reader,

Let me say a few words about what I had in mind when I wrote this book.

Assuming, you are creative and innovative entrepreneurs and want to have an impact with your work, it's all about YOU. As a consultant in the creative industries and social entrepreneurship I highly identify with my clients and partners, with their values and attitudes, their way of thinking and acting. To build up an appreciative and personal relationship is part of my practice. This book I regard as another way of building relationships. Therefore, I mostly address you personally, in the second person, and some-times I even chose the first-person plural, when it feels like you are sitting next to me or we share the same ideas and concerns.

Whether you work in one of the creative industries – like archi-tecture, design, fashion, communication, etc. – or in the growing field of social entrepreneurship, whether you are a single entre-preneur or a small to medium enterprise, whether you are just starting out or already in the business for years, the topic of strat-egy is equally important and the contents of the book are valid.

Values and attitudes are often reflected by the way our work-spaces look. The photos in the book are illustrations of some of these creative workspaces, and were all taken by me. Also, I made all the sketches and diagrams myself. They are my per-sonal interpretation and adaption of existing tools and methods, and I work with them regularly.

Since the German edition of the book some new tools and methods for social impact-oriented modeling and reporting have been created and provided. Some I included in the English edition, as I find them extremely important. They, in my opinion, not only work in the field of social entrepreneurship, but help in general to turn your ideas into change-making strategies, shifting yours and your client's perspective.

Hope you enjoy!

Doris Rothauer

1

What is
and

Strategy
Why?

"Strategy, it turns out, is one of those words that people define in one way and often use in another, without realizing the difference."

HENRY MINTZBERG, 1987

A Catch-22?

In a profit-driven world, where economic growth is merely based on efficiency instead of effectiveness, the term strategy seems to be one of the most used empty words. We tend to use it liberally without knowing what it really means. Having a strategy seems to be an imperative and a success formula per se. Even worse, when strategy is mixed up with unethical or opportunistic tactics. For example, if you come up with some clever maneuvering to override others for your own advantage. And finally, in an entrepreneurial context, strategy is often misunderstood as a business plan filling pages and pages of numbers and odd texts that leave no space for creativity and innovation.

In fact, strategy should be a creative meaningful process, designing a sustainable future based on clear visions, values and attitudes. This is, what we desperately need in our profit-driven world in order to change it for the better – be it on a personal or a business level. And, this is how we will look at strategy in the following pages.

Visions Need Strategies

Visions are the driving force for social innovation and we need to have visions in order to be able to create and evolve. But, without a strategy on how to achieve our vision, the vision stays a vision and consequently will have zero impact. Therefore, visions need strategies. Working with creative and social entrepreneurs, I often experience the lack of strategic thinking and so a lot of creative energy is wasted without leading to success. The way is the goal, or the journey is the reward – sayings attributed to Confucius –, and strategy means designing this journey deliberately.

Moreover, vision and strategy should enhance each other: Not only do visions need strategies – strategies need to be based on visions in order to be powerful.

"Always remember that this whole thing was started with a mouse."

WALT DISNEY

Business development without following a visionary strategy leaves the future to chance. In times where complexity and the pace of change is constantly rising this does not work anymore. The same applies to relying on success stories of the past. As entrepreneurs, we need to reinvent ourselves almost every day and yet stick to our visions.

⊠ [1] WHAT HAPPENS TO GREAT IDEAS, MOTMOT DESIGN

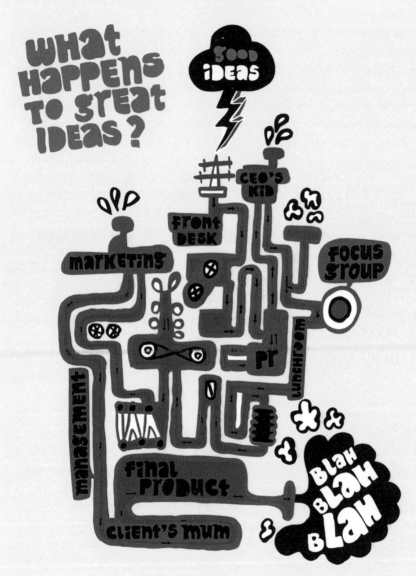

This Book

This book helps to understand the connection between strategy and vision, strategy and creativity and strategy and innovative thinking, all based on values and attitudes. It follows an approach to strategy as a meaningful, playful, experimental and therefore creative way to design your future, your (social) impact and, at the same time, be economically successful.

From all the different theories and approaches in strategic management that I have compiled and interpreted, these are, from my experience, the most valuable, especially for creative and social entrepreneurs. The mix of methods and tools, that I provide in the second half of the book, are based on my work as a systemic consultant. Whether you are a single entrepreneur or small to medium enterprise, just starting or already in the market in a creative industry like architecture, design, fashion, music, or in the social impact business, you are addressed equally.

The book is structured in four parts, starting with a basic introduction into my approach to strategy, followed by a description of the process of strategic development. Included in the third part are the 10 most helpful tips when going through this process. The fourth part of the book is set out to be a workbook, providing you with a selection of tools and methods that you can apply to your own business development.

⊠ [2] THE STRATEGY PYRAMID

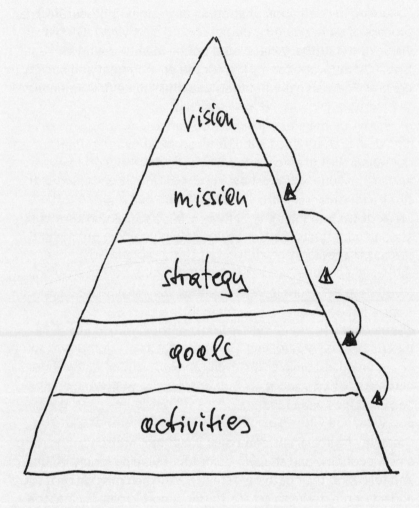

A Top-Down Approach

Following my definition of strategy as designing the future, the process of developing strategies should start with having a clear vision of the future: What would be the ideal situation in the future – for my work, for my life, for the environment and society in general. The vision is what fuels you, the source of your energy.

A clear vision manifests in a mission, answering the "why" – why am I doing what I do. It's the purpose of our work, our business, our being. The strategy lays out the "how" – how do I best achieve my why. It is a general layout, a kind of road map, that takes a lot of factors into consideration. From there you can break down the goals and activities. It is a top down approach, starting with the vision on top, ending with a spectrum of activities at the bottom.

If you develop your business the other way around, you are trapped in what can be described as "empty": not being clear about what you stand for. The basis of the pyramid, the activities, might and should change over time, as part of a constant adaptive development. The vision as well as the mission should always guide you and therefore not change, becoming clearer and clearer as you move on.

Creative and social entrepreneurs are at the forefront of building a new economy and shaping our future by being highly visionary and following their path persistently. May their mission be a social impact or the desire to create, to bring more creativity into the world, they are mostly value-driven instead of profit-driven. Turbulences and obstacles are regarded as challenges. Challenges, that need strategies to be overcome.

Comparing Strategy to a Safari

In his bestseller "Strategy Safari" (1998) the author Henry Mintzberg, who is one of the leading and most creative thinkers on business and management, takes us on a journey through "the wilds of strategic management", as the subtitle proposes. In his context, the wilds are the many different approaches and theories, that exist in the academic business world and that show how bewildering the term and concept of strategy can be if you need guidelines. Mintzberg and his co-authors narrow them down to ten major schools of strategic management, depicting a comprehensive and powerful overview.

The metaphor of a safari perfectly fits to how you could approach and develop strategic thinking. Whoever has been on a real safari will have experienced the mind-blowing fascination of a wilderness, that in its minimalistic vastness forces you to sharpen your eye and focus on details. On a single tree, a single animal, a subtle noise or movement. Details, that can develop an enormous appeal as well as a danger. In this wilderness, no one can survive without a strategy – whether it's a human, an animal or a plant.

There is another aspect in strategy development that is comparable to a journey and is, in my opinion, crucial, especially if you aim at being innovative: The openness for experiments and improvisation. If you go on a journey, it is impossible to plan every little detail perfectly ahead. On the contrary, what makes a journey an awesome experience, are all the discoveries off the beaten track. Strategy is like a safari: You need to develop an attentive mind and pay attention to details around you, and you need to think outside the box.

How It All Started

The term strategy originates from the Greek language, combining *stratós* (army) and *ágo* (lead). In ancient Greece, someone who was officially appointed to lead the army was called a strategist. The military connotation evokes a well-known picture in our head: that of a commander standing on the top of a hill overlooking the open country and observing all movements, of his army as well as the enemy's army.

The earliest known writing on military strategy goes back to ancient China, to Sun Tzu, a Chinese general and philosopher, who lived around 500 BC. His most influential work, "The Art of War", continues to be cited and referred to by political and business leaders up to the present, not least thanks to its philosophical ideas introducing a Taoist approach.

Much later in history, another influential military strategist was the Prussian general Carl von Clausewitz and his treatise "On War", published in 1832, shortly after his death. Besides his elaborate distinction between strategy and tactics he is most known for his ideas on the relationship between war and politics. His assumption that war is merely the continuation of politics by other means is a relevant topic to date.

In our context, I recommend his principle of building a strategy on strengthening your strengths – or, in other words, knowing and focusing on your core competencies. More about that later.

"The best strategy is always to be very strong, first generally, then at the decisive point. Therefore, (...) there is no more imperative and simpler law for strategy than to keep the forces concentrated."

CARL VON CLAUSEWITZ, ON WAR III, 11

From the military concepts of strategy to strategy as a business and management approach it took until the 1950ies, when the Harvard Business School first introduced the term into their management education. Meanwhile, there are dozens of different theories of strategic management.

Strategic Thinking Versus Strategic Planning

"The best strategies are visions, not plans."

HENRY MINTZBERG, 1994

Most of these theories, dating back to the 20th century, at the height of industrialization, focused on the planning aspect of strategy. At present, in a globalized economy, we are confronted with an ever-growing complexity and constantly changing environments. The future is unpredictable, even the near future. Therefore, designing the future merely based on numerical data and analysis doesn't work anymore. We need to develop a strategic thinking instead of planning, that is adaptive to changes. This requires a more experimental and creative approach. It means to constantly observe everything around us, be reflective, identify chances that are worth seizing, and mix and match boldly. Therefore, strategic thinking corresponds to an entrepreneurial mindset. This is a big advantage for you as a creative or social entrepreneur! Just be aware of it.

Henry Mintzberg, to whom I frequently refer, was one of the first economists who stressed the importance of strategic thinking and the difference to planning: "Planning has always been about analysis. (…) Strategic thinking, in contrast, is about synthesis. It involves intuition and creativity." (Mintzberg, 1995)

All your knowledge, skills and experience, your values and attitudes are part of the synthesis, that Mintzberg addresses. Strategic thinking is a mindset as well as a learning process. It's about balancing continuity and change, about evolving from reflective learning.

To be able to reflect, it might be necessary and even advisable, every now and then, to step back from daily business and take some devoted time for evaluation and creation. Typically, this can be organized as a workshop or in some other kind of exclusive setting. At the same time, strategic thinking as a mindset can and should be internalized in our daily routine. Whatever we do, even the slightest decisions and actions, should be done and reflected in the context of our larger goals. Plus, thinking ahead as part of our routine helps to act more strategically. An easy exercise is to incorporate this in the weekly to-do-list and planer: an invitation for a networking lunch, an evening event to join, other sources of inspiration to watch out for, and – crucially – deciding what to leave out, where to say no. Because strategic thinking is also about focusing and selecting.

Creativity and Impact

A key element in strategic thinking is creativity. In our profit-driven economy we have for a long time excluded all forms of creativity in the working world. We have lived up to paradigms, that are the opposite to creativity, in order to perform efficiently and increase productivity just for profit's sake. That's why strategy was mostly understood as planning, based on measurability and predictability. But times have changed. We experience a massive crisis as well as transformation of economy and society, and the paradigms of the industrial age don't work anymore. What we need now is a new innovative way of thinking and problem solving, based on creativity and flexibility.

"Creativity involves putting your imagination to work."

KEN ROBINSON, 2011

✉ [3] BEND THE RULES, DESIGNED BY ARASH AND KELLY

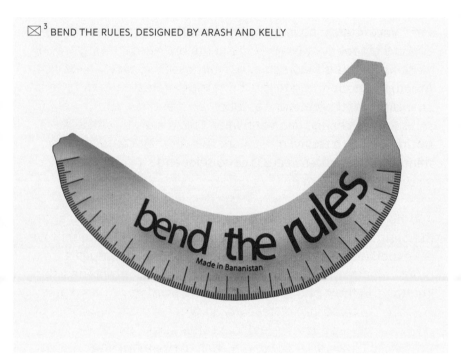

To foster creativity, we don't need to be artists, but we can de-velop an artistic mindset: change the perspective, think outside the box, question our patterns and habits, challenge our imag-ination, experiment with the unknown, connect things in a new or unusual way, be open minded, passionate and curious. The science of neurology has, in the last 10 to 15 years, uncovered some very interesting insights into how the creative mind works. One is that creativity is a process in the brain based on balancing tensions: tensions between chaos and order, spontaneity and structure, freedom and discipline, imagination and reality, im-provisation and perfection, emotion and rationality, uncertainty and security, change and continuity. This is exactly what we are confronted with today in our work, in everyday life. We con-stantly find ourselves in areas of conflict and stress. Creativity is crucial to deal with it.

Another expression of creativity is the creation of meaning and the desire for impact. This again conforms to a paradigm shift we are experiencing, more and more, in our economy: the shift from profit-orientation to impact-orientation. Social entrepreneurship is at the forefront of this new development.

Creative and Social Entrepreneurship

When talking about strategic thinking, creativity and flexibility, vision and impact, the term "entrepreneurship" often comes up. In the last decade, we have seen an enormous hype around entrepreneurship. New business models and innovative busi-ness strategies are merely emerging from small and medium size companies, who are a driving force of the new economies. They change the way we work, live, consume. Through digitalization, all these "little islands", that pop up everywhere in the world, can

interconnect with each other and reach out to like-minded individuals and communities, according to their values and mission.

The innovative type of an entrepreneur goes back to the Austrian-American economist Alois Joseph Schumpeter (1883–1950), who, in the 1930s, defined an entrepreneur as one of combining various input factors in an innovative manner to generate new value to the customer. The innovation can aim at new goods, new techniques, new markets or new organizational structures. The entrepreneur becomes the revolutionary, upsetting the established order to create dynamic change. Schumpeter's famous term "creative destruction" suggests that entrepreneurial innovation and experimentation constantly destroy the old and introduce new economic equilibria. Schumpeter himself was a revolutionary. Teaching at Harvard, at a time when economic science developed along static and mathematically oriented equilibrium models, he broke with the tradition. Later in the 20th century, his theory of relating entrepreneurship to innovation was long time forgotten, until recently. In 2000 the US-magazine Business Week titled him "America's hottest economist". His idea of an entrepreneur has since entered the mainstream.

Today, we see another interpretation of an entrepreneur being the revolutionary: the social entrepreneur. Driven by an innovative idea that can help solve the most pressing problems society is facing today, the social entrepreneur aims at systemic change – that is a change in patterns in a specific field, industry, or across society. One of the first to recognize and support the importance of social entrepreneurship was Bill Drayton, the founder of Ashoka. His vision, that everyone can and must be a changemaker, has come to live through a whole new generation of entrepreneurs and their ecosystems, being one of the strongest movements in the massive transformation of our economy and society we are experiencing today.

"Entrepreneurs cannot be happy people until they have seen their visions become the new reality across all of society."

BILL DRAYTON

With their creative skills and abilities, creative entrepreneurs are contributing a powerful part to the changemaker world. Mostly working in one of the creative industries, they are driven by values and attitudes more than by profit. Their artistic mindset and out-of-the-box-thinking enables them to experiment with expression, shift our perception, raise awareness and find new, creative ways of problem solving in a world, that desperately needs more creativity.

The Systemic Approach

Finally, we take a short excursion into systems theory and its application on strategic thinking. Remember the picture of the commander on top of the hill? To better analyze and understand yourself and everything around you – your "system" and the surrounding "systems" –, you need to step out and put yourself in the "helicopter perspective" or "bird's eye view". Only from there you can see and take every aspect into consideration and integrate it into the whole picture. Systemic thinking can thus enhance strategic thinking and development.

In systems theory, a system is characterized by its ability to live and survive, no matter what threatens its existence. The systemic approach in strategic thinking and management looks at every organization as a living organism, that follows its evolutionary path, adapting to changes, whether from within or outside. It's a permanent process of communication and decisions guided by its own patterns, its *modus operandi*. Strategic development is about maximizing the viability and not the profit. Many of the tools and methods provided in the fourth chapter of the book, are systemic tools. They help you get into the bird's eye view and see the whole picture as well as activate your potential for self-steering, especially if you are a small company or single entrepreneur.

2

How to
Strat

Develop
egies

The Process of Developing Strategies

Developing strategies is a process based on three principles:
it should be structured, it needs time (off) and it is a reflexive
process.

As we said earlier, *strategic thinking* as a mindset can and should
be internalized in our daily routine. But, *evaluating* your business strategies and *developing* new ones should not be a topic
on your daily agenda, in the weekly meeting between 10–11 am,
or in the lunch break. For this, you need to step back from daily
business and take some devoted time. Typically, this can be organized as a workshop or in some other kind of exclusive setting, following a structured agenda and moderation, and ideally
supported by tools and methods.

⊠ [4] THE PROCESS OF DEVELOPING STRATEGIES AS A REFLEXIVE LOOP

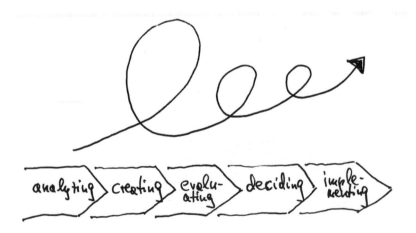

analyzing ⟩ creating ⟩ evalu-ating ⟩ deciding ⟩ imple-menting

Analyzing and Identifying

To begin with, you analyze your starting point, from all different kinds of views: the internal view on yourself and your company – vision, values, resources, competencies –, the external view on your clients, the market, the stakeholders, the ecosystem, and – last but not least – the bigger view on the economy and society in general. The more you take in consideration, the more holistic you look at the present and the future, the more impact you will create.

Here's a list of possible questions that may serve you as a framework:

○ What is my / our vision?
○ What values do I / we stand for?
○ What topics, challenges and (social) problems do I / we want to adress?
○ What impact do I / we want to achieve?
○ What resources do I / we dispose of?
○ What core competencies do I / we bring in? What is my / our expertise?
○ In what market / enviroment / ecosystem do I / we act?
○ What are the rules, paradigms and dynamics of my / our field of business?
○ Who are my / our clients / beneficiaries / stakeholders / partners / communities?
○ What are their expectations and needs?
○ What changes in our market / enviroment / in society in general do I / we observe?

Henry Mintzberg, whom you know already from the first chapter, described strategic thinking also as *seeing* – seeing from different perspectives. In his analogy of a bridge he identifies seven perspectives you should consider:

1 Looking back: Where do I / we come from, what are the lessons from the past, which strategies worked so far, which not?

2 Seeing from above: Take an overview and see the big picture, including trends, risks and chances in the market.

3 Seeing below: Identify the necessary resources and skills, analyze your financial data (costs and sales) as well as your strengths and weaknesses.

4 Seeing ahead: Focus on the future – What are possible scenarios?

5 Looking besides: What are my / our benchmarks, what strategies do they pursue?

6 Looking beyond: What is my / our vision, what do I / we aim for, even if it is not realizable now?

7 Seeing through: Implement your strategies!

⊠ [5] THE SEVEN PERSPECTIVES OF STRATEGIC THINKING ACCORDING TO MINTZBERG
(SOURCE: ORGANISATIONSENTWICKLUNG, ISSUE 4 / 2007)

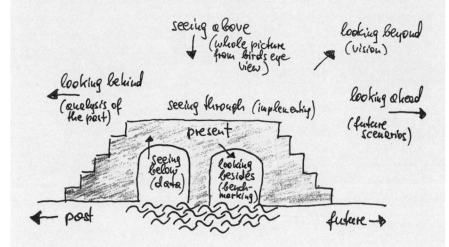

Creating and Experimenting

The analysis provides you with important information, insights, views, assumptions and challenges. Now, as a next step, the creative part of developing strategies comes into play: Combining all the gathered factors, potentials and chances you can create ideas and possible scenarios and design future options and solutions. It is an experimental approach, a mix and match of factors and ideas. You can think about new areas of expertise, new products and services, new markets, new cooperation projects, new networks, and even new organizational structures within your own organization. You can think about diversifying or focusing, growing or downsizing, scaling or pooling – the more options you create, the more innovative the results will be. For those, who want to be changemakers, you should think about what would trigger a systemic change and if scaling is the next option.

Evaluating, Deciding and Fine-Tuning

As part of the reflexive process, you need to evaluate all the options before you can decide which to pursue. Comparing the options with your vision, your values, your core competencies helps you to clearly see where you identify most, what makes your heart sing. At the same time, you should also take the time and effort for a kind of assessment – that is "looking below" as we defined it in Mintzberg's Strategy Bridge: Looking at your resources, capabilities and finances and evaluate what is most feasible. Fine-tuning means to think it well through – what are the details, what are the consequences.

In an article for the Harvard Business Review from 1987 Mintzberg compares developing strategies with "crafting", based on skills, dedication, involvement, experience, mastery of details and creativity. In his metaphor of a potter, managers are craftsman and strategy is their clay. "At work, the potter sits before a lump of clay on the wheel. Her mind is on the clay, but she is also aware of sitting between her past experiences and her future prospects. She knows exactly what has and has not worked for her in the past. She has an intimate knowledge of her work, her capabilities, and her markets. As a craftsman, she senses rather than analyzes these things; her knowledge is "tacit." All these things are working in her mind as her hands are working the clay. The product that emerges on the wheel is likely to be in the tradition of her past work, but she may break away and embark on a new direction. Even so, the past is no less present, projecting itself into the future." (Henry Mintzberg, 1987)

Planning and Implementing

A strategy is only a strategy when it is implemented and lived as well. As long as it is just on paper, it's a concept. Implementing requires planning, finally: planning the activities, the resources, the finances, the timing, the organizational structure. Plans, that need to be integrated and incorporated in your daily business routine. Establishing a strategic controlling is part of the planning (controlling the planning) as well as the reflexive approach in the process (evaluating the outcome). What has been done, what remains to be done, what is successful, what not, what is supportive, what not, what has an impact, what not, etc. Questions and answers that may lead to adaptions in the planning and – potentially – in your strategies. Welcome back in the loop.

In the fourth and last chapter of the book you will find a useful collection of tools and methods, that support the process of developing strategies, mainly in the analyzing and creating phase.

Prior to that, I collected the 10 most valuable assumptions and tips serving as a guidance and framework when developing strategies. Some we have already mentioned. They have, from my experience as a consultant, proved to apply especially for creative and social entrepreneurs.

ABOUT   WO

ANSWERS   NE

K   PRESS

S   STORE

3

10 Assu
and
as a Gu

ptions
Tips
dance

$$\boxed{1}$$

To Be Future-Oriented

Despite having all the perspectives in mind, the focus should be forward-looking and future-oriented. One reason is your vision, and your goal to manifest your vision, step by step, so that it becomes a reality. Being future-oriented means being visionary. And successful strategies follow visions. Another reason is the condition of our world, that is continuously changing. It's the engine for development, the purpose of being innovative. Businesses, who only rely on success stories of the past and don't move ahead, are at risk. The same applies to problem-solving. The way problems were solved in the past, might not work any longer in the future. To foster development and innovation, you need to be future-oriented. A quote from the Canadian ice hockey legend Wayne Gretzky puts it in a nutshell: "Skate to where the puck is going to be, not where it has been."

MY TIP

Be curious, be attentive! Observe your scene, your colleagues, the news, social media, conferences, literature, art and other influential and inspiring sources of interest. What are the drivers of change? Particularly creative and social entrepreneurs have an intuitive feeling for future needs and trends. Make this a core competence.

"Life can only be understood backwards; but it must be lived forwards."

SØREN KIERKEGAARD

$$\boxed{2}$$

To Be Impact-Oriented

In a world, that is drastically confronted with inequality and exploitation of resources we need to reconsider our economic strategies and the way we work together. So far, business models have been profit-driven, mainly focusing on an ever-growing *output,* but not on the *outcome* – that is the impact the output has on the organization, the target groups, on society in general.

Creative and social entrepreneurs mostly have a different motivation and approach. They want to create some sort of impact with their work, they want to change something for the better, change people's awareness, values and attitudes, thinking and acting. They are generally impact-oriented. Remember: the best strategies are visions. But also: the best strategies are impact strategies!

MY TIP

The social entrepreneurship movement has developed tools and methods how to create impact business models, how to evaluate the impact and how to scale and transfer the impact. They help you create sustainable, impactful strategies. Some of these tools and their resources you'll find in the fourth chapter.

PEOPLE ARE chang world.

$$\boxed{3}$$

To Build on Your Values, Strengths and Competencies

20th century management theory has developed two different approaches to strategy: the market-based view and the resource-based view.

The market based view is, as the name proposes, based on the market: The success of a business is determined by external factors, that is by the customers and their behavior, by the competitors and their moves, by the trends on the market, by the structure of the specific sector, etc. It is a very competitive approach. The resource-based view concentrates on recognizing and utilizing the organizations resources and abilities. For entrepreneurs, this includes their values, culture, skills, strengths and core competencies, even their passion and devotion, that makes them thrive. I recommend building your strategies on these internal factors. This allows you to create impact over mere profit, think and act in co-operations and networks and identify with what you are doing. It aims at creating the future together with like-minded partners and communities, each contributing to a common vision with their individual strengths and competencies.

MY TIP

One of your core competencies is your creativity. In every step you make, use and foster your creativity, not only for your customers and beneficiaries sake, but for your personal development and potential as well.

"Everyone has the perfect gift to give the world-and if each of us is freed up to give our unique gift, the world will be in total harmony."

BUCKMINSTER FULLER

4

To Pursue Opportunities

The Austrian-American economist Peter Drucker, often referred to as the father of modern management, has left us with some simple and yet most effective thoughts on management and strategy, that are true more than ever. In his opinion, the catalyst for innovation is not so much the search for new products, but the will to change the environment. You might know the saying a glass is half full or half empty. So, depending on how you look at it, any change can either be a threat or an opportunity. When you analyze the market and the environment, it is therefore advisable to identify those chances and opportunities, that could trigger positive change. If you then combine your strengths and competencies with those opportunities, you will very likely create effective and innovative strategies.

MY TIP

If you follow Mahatma Gandhi's "Be the change you want to see in the world", then you will see and take opportunities exactly where you want to see them.

"Don't solve problems. Pursue opportunities."

PETER DRUCKER

5

To Deeply Understand Your Clients
and Beneficiaries

The more you understand your clients and beneficiaries, the more purposeful you can create your offer. "Understand" means know their story, their needs and desires, their values, lifestyle, culture, background. With business clients, you should know as much as possible about their business, not only what is obvious and officially communicated, but what is under the surface. Creatives, especially in the field of design, often act as consultants, digging deep into the culture and organization of the client.

Knowing and understanding your clients and beneficiaries does not subsequently mean living up to their expectations. It means identifying, sharing, exchanging and cooperating with them. Be open to learning from each other. It's a sympathetic and cooperative approach rather than "I sell you buy". You can even co-create solutions, involve them actively in your story, and make their story your challenge.

MY TIP

Especially with creative and social entrepreneurs, target groups not only buy or profit from their innovative products, services and solutions, but also want to share and participate in their values and missions. So, make sure by understanding your clients and beneficiaries that their values match yours.

6

To Ask the Right Questions

In the process of developing strategies, whether you are analyzing, creating or evaluating, asking the right questions is crucial. "Right" means relevant, like questions that generate new
information and insights instead of just testing existing data, or
questions that examine something from different points of view.
The idea is to open your mind, shift your perspective, make you
reflect and speculate, question purpose and context, enable
and support creative and experimental thinking.

Relevant has another dimension too. In strategic thinking and
questioning – and in life in general – it should not be about
judging if something is right or wrong, it should be about re-
flecting if things could be done differently. Instead of asking *Am
I doing things right?* you could ask *Am I doing the right things?*
This implies that it could be done differently, which aims at
purpose, effectiveness and impact.

— MY TIP —
For creating innovative scenarios, a simple technique is the
"What-if" question, where you go really wild …

"Efficiency is concerned with doing things right, effective- ness is doing the right things."

PETER DRUCKER, 1967

$$\boxed{7}$$

To Take the Helicopter View

We talked about this more in depth in the first chapter. The view from above helps to see the whole picture as well as the single pieces, the present as well as the past and the future, your own system as well as the surrounding systems. Ideally, looking from above, you may find connections that are new, that you have not seen or missed before. In addition, it supports positioning your work in the greater context of society. Strategic thinking from the helicopter view is seeing the world as one big network, with many possibilities to hook in.

MY TIP

Don't spend too much time only on your desk or your computer. To get authentic input for the big picture as well as the details, you need to go out into the real world, where you want to see your outcome and impact.

"The desk is a
dangerous place
from which to
view the world."

JOHN LE CARRÉ

To Take Some Time-Out

Another issue, we have already touched here and there: Developing strategies needs time and space. To see the big picture, you need to step back from daily business, otherwise *you don't see the forest through the trees.* Moreover, time-out and breaks foster creativity. Long time common knowledge, neurology has meanwhile proven that when you are stuck with a problem, the flashing idea comes only after you let go. Some innovative companies have obligatory time-out for their creative heads, where they can experiment with whatever they want. For the process of developing strategies, the devoted time-out should still be structured and supported by tools and methods.

MY TIP

Don't underestimate the time for implementing, which is also extra time, at least in the beginning.

$$\boxed{9}$$

To Follow the Reflexive Loop

Apropos timing: Developing strategies is not a one-time duty. It needs a reflexive approach and the awareness, that parameters and conditions can change any time. The flexibility to adapt your strategies is an important key to success. This flexibility should not only be a reaction to changes in the environment. As part of a strategic thinking, you should develop a critical spirit, always questioning what you are doing, if it is still the right thing, the right strategy. Analyzing, creating and evaluating, seizing chances and opportunities, developing new ideas and evaluating what works and what not is an ongoing process to keep in the flow.

MY TIP

"Institutionalize" this reflexive process by implementing regularly strategy sessions or workshops, at least once a year.

10

To Make Strategic Thinking a Mind Set

The importance of strategic thinking over strategic planning
has been made clear already. The importance of strategic thinking as a general mindset follows the same argument. In a fast
changing, challenging and complex world we need to be alert,
curious, creative, open minded, flexible. We need to be visionary, empathic, authentic, mindful. We need to observe, analyze,
experiment, create, evaluate, decide, act. All this is supported by
strategic thinking – and vice versa, strategic thinking supports all
these skills and attitudes. We need to develop a holistic picture
of what we are doing and what is our contribution to the world –
a picture, that consists of many little details and elements that
should be carefully and responsibly designed, with special effort
on the connecting parts.

MY TIP

Developing strategies and strategic thinking is not quite the
same, but they condition each other. Be aware of that.

TODA

28

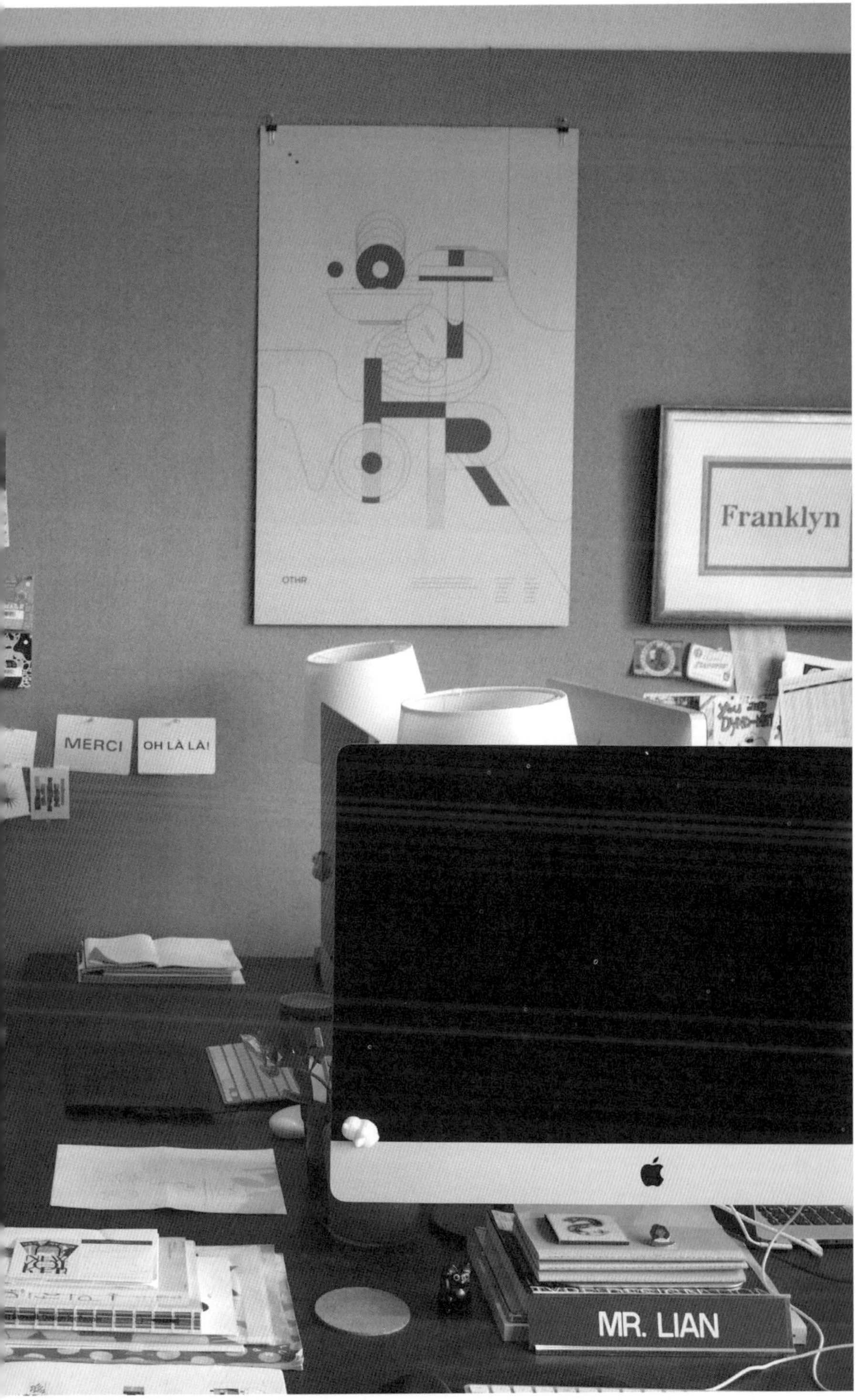
OTHR
Franklyn
MERCI
OH LÀ LÀ!
MR. LIAN

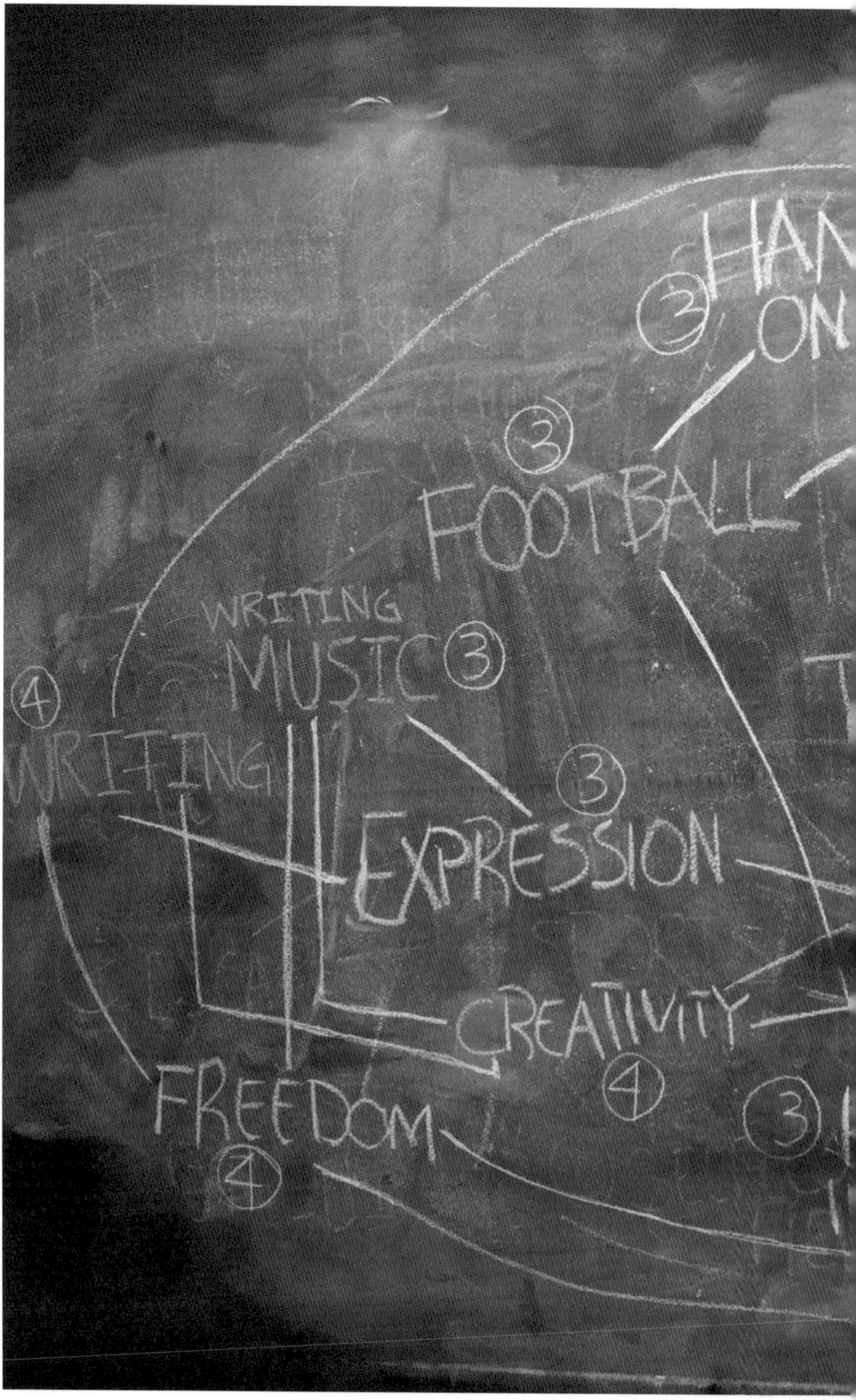

FOOTBALL
WRITING
MUSIC
WRITING
EXPRESSION
CREATIVITY
FREEDOM

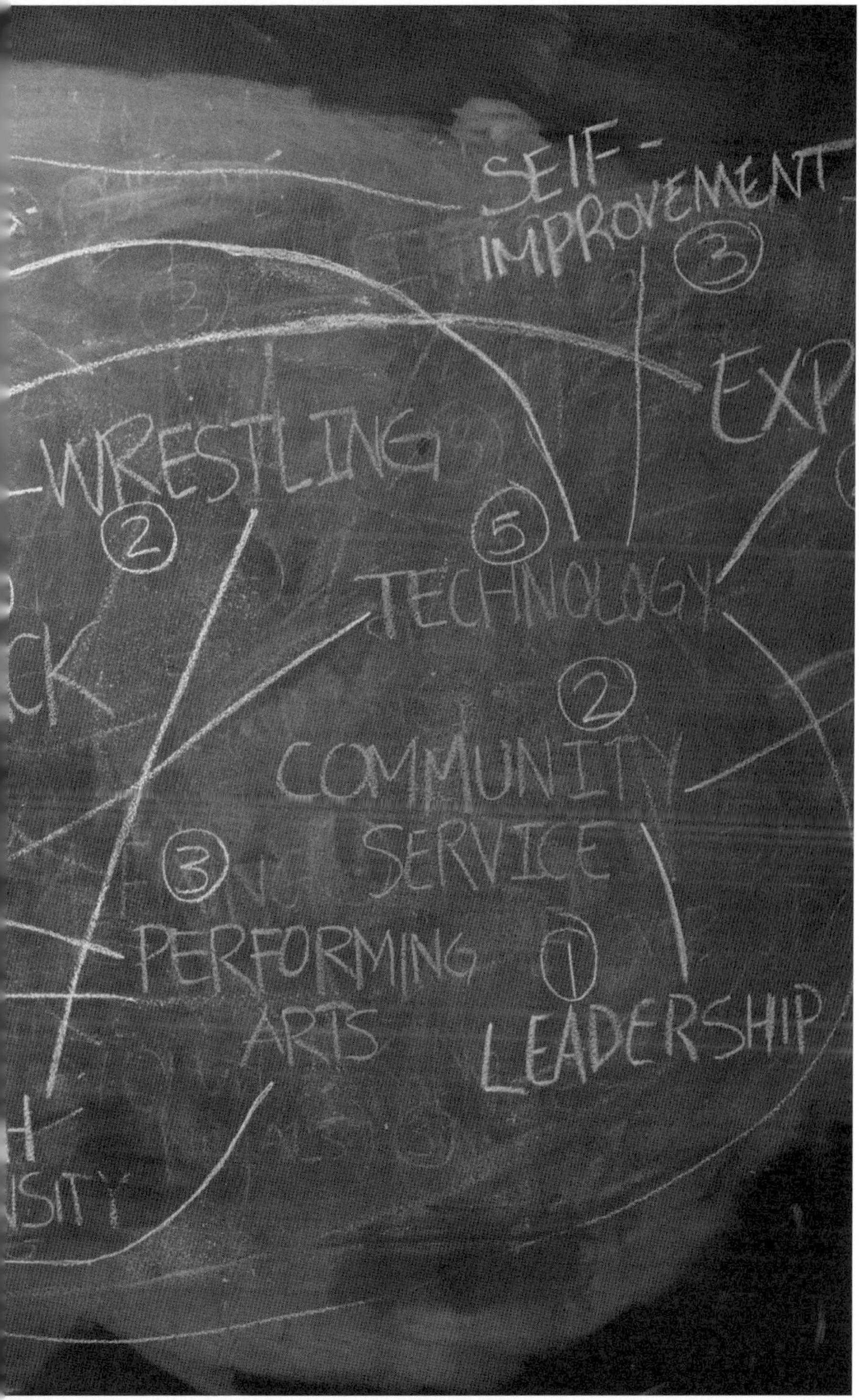
SELF-
IMPROVEMENT
3
EXP
WRESTLING
2
5
TECHNOLOGY
CK
2
COMMUNITY
SERVICE
3
PERFORMING
ARTS
1
LEADERSHIP
H
SITY

4

Tool
Met

and
ods

How to Use the Tools

The tools and methods I provide are a selection, based on my experience, work and systemic approach, that you can choose from and experiment with, per your individual needs. There is no strict order to follow, but with every tool, you'll find a reference to the phase in which it is recommended, and explanations on the context. With this workbook, I am mostly focusing on tools and methods for analyzing and creating. Implementing is not part of it, since this affects the operational aspects and planning.

Included are some new tools and methods for social impact-oriented modeling and reporting, that I find extremely important and helpful for turning visions and ideas into change-making strategies.

Some of the systemic tools come out of the so-called "Viennese School of Management Consultancy", developed in the late 1990s, as a united effort of social scientists, business administrators and consultants, group-dynamics therapists and psychoanalysts. Their aim was to offer alternative approaches to organizational development and change theories, at a time, when classical approaches increasingly failed.

I advise you to develop an experimental approach, checking out several tools and methods, even on the same issue, to get the whole picture from different perspectives. Moreover, this will train your strategic *thinking.*

Starting Point and Goals

Before you start the process, make sure to know where you start from: What is my business? Where do I stand with it? What's the motivation and goal of the process? What should be different afterwards?

If your business has been running for a while, it might just be about evaluating and adopting, or about something completely new. It might be driven by necessity and pressure, or curiosity and the wish to innovate. If you are starting a new business, you need to make sure you have a clear business model that follows your vision, your competences, capacities and the needs among your target group. If you are a team, you need to make sure that everyone is in the same boat and that you share a common understanding of the starting point and goals.

The following tools will help you find your starting point.

TOOL

$$\boxed{1}$$

DEFINING A BUSINESS MODEL

Source: Peter Drucker

PHASE

Starting point, when you evaluate your existing business model or create a new one.

TOPIC

Knowing what your core business is.

HOW TO APPLY

A business model is based on three pillars and their relationship to each other: WHAT do I do for WHOM and HOW (SEE ILL. 6).

"WHAT" DESCRIBES:
○ What is the purpose of my business?
○ What is my offer (service or product)?
○ In what industry / sector / area am I operating?
○ What is the benefit / impact of my offer?

FOR "WHOM" DESCRIBES:
○ Who is my target group?
○ What is their profile?
○ What are their needs?
○ What do they value?
○ What characterizes the market?

⊠ 6 DEFINITION OF A BUSINESS MODEL

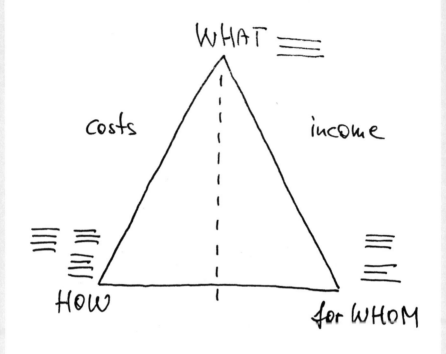

"HOW" DESCRIBES:
◦ How do I create and deliver my offer?
◦ What skills, competencies and resources do I need for it?
◦ What activities are involved?
◦ Who are my key partners?

The "HOW" involves costs, the "WHO" creates income, therefore the business model should also define the cost structure and revenue model.

TIP

The business model is a clear picture in your head, that you should be able to describe in three sentences. You can draw it on a poster with icons and key words, making it comprehensible. You can also check out the popular "Business Model Canvas" by Alex Osterwalder, which is based on Drucker's business model description.

COMMENT

Be aware that a business *model* is not a business *plan*. A business model creates an overall picture and definition of what your business is. A business plan is a detailed description of every aspect, including marketing activities and distribution, an analysis of the risks and the competition, a financial plan and budget for the next 3–5 years and a time schedule. It's a written document on 15–20 pages, mostly required by banks and business angels.

Also, a business model is not a strategy, but the basis for strategies. It can, for example, result in a business model innovation (SEE P. 137 / TOOL 16 – BUSINESS MODEL INNOVATION).

A slightly different approach to business models are impact models, that focus on solving a social problem, and are thus not output- but outcome-oriented (SEE P. 112 / TOOL 9 – IMPACT MODEL).

TOOL

2

CHANGE MAP

Source: Barbara Heitger, Alexander Doujak

PHASE

Starting point, when there is a need or will to change.

TOPIC

The Change Map helps to identify the kind and extent of change that might be necessary or favored, and the direction it should go, especially when there is uncertainty or anxiety for it within a team.

HOW TO APPLY

Everyone in a team gives his / her personal estimate about where he / she thinks the team stands regarding the capability and the necessity for change, by making a mark on the map (ILL. 7) . Analyze and discuss the results, if it is about mobilizing, learning, securing, survival or repositioning and renewal.

Mobilizing means increasing the capacity and willingness for change. Learning means continuous development. For learning organizations change is day to day business. Securing survival means focusing on surviving and decreasing the current need for change. Repositioning and renewal can be any form of pro-active strategic turnaround and / or growth.

⊠ 7 CHANGE MAP

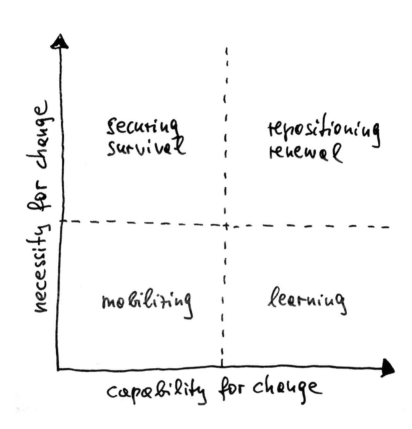

Vision

"We are all in the gutter, but some of us are looking at the stars."

OSCAR WILDE

What a perfect quote to describe what it means to be visionary. Be it on a personal or on a business level, having a vision can develop a magnetic attraction and overwhelming desire, like a shining star. A star, that guides us and fuels our motivation and energy. We know from history, that visionary entrepreneurs and leaders have contributed to major changes in technology, economy and society. Just imagine Henry Ford and his vision of a car industry at a time, when horse-drawn carriages filled the streets. Or Steve Jobs and his vision of a user-friendly computer in every home, at every desk, at a time when computers were huge machines taking up a whole room and a science all its own.

In the business context, a vision is often described as an ideal business goal that is currently not realizable, but is nevertheless being aimed for. It's a challenging idea for the future, and the fact that it is a challenge makes it a driving force. The direction is clear, the strategy should leave room for development and change.

Within a team a vision combines forces, gives orientation, enables identification and supports motivation. It's not about goals in term of deadlines and numbers, but about emotions, pictures in your head. It's about the purpose of working and living.

IMPACT HUB NYC

Welcome

Please check in

RECEPTION

TOOL

3

QUESTIONNAIRE

- Where does my energy and motivation come from?
- What is my big plan, my picture of an ideal future?
- What problems do I want to solve, what change do I want to create and see?
- What impact should my work have on my environment, on society?
- What kind of life do I want to live?
- What is the ideal work to live that life?
- Where do I want to be in 10 years?
- How do I want to be perceived in 10 years from my environment, from the people I work for and with?
- What metaphor or picture comes to mind to describe my vision?

TOOL

4

LOOKING BACK FROM THE FUTURE

Source: Alexander Exner, Roswita Königswieser

PHASE

Analyzing and creating.

TOPIC

This playful exercise helps to create a picture of the future by activating your imagination and creativity and opening your mind.

HOW TO APPLY

It is a role play, that simulates a fictitious interview between two people. They can be anyone from your team or you and a counterpart. The situation takes place in 10 years from now, when your vision is reality. The interviewee is the one who achieved his / her vision, the interviewer makes a report about the success story, asking how it was achieved, what were the obstacles, the strategy, the milestones, etc. Take a few minutes to prepare and then act.

TIP
Document the questions and answers, as they usually bring up some helpful hints on possible strategies, even if they were "invented" spontaneously.

Mission and Culture

If the *vision* is a design, a draft, a plan of the future, the *mission* is the deriving statement, that declares what it is all about. It describes what you stand for, why you do what you do. It's the purpose of your work. It reflects the values and attitudes that are important for you, the impact you strive for, the outcome you want to achieve. It is the result of analyzing yourself and your business, the entrepreneurial self-understanding, driven by your vision. It is an important part and communication tool of your strategy. As a written statement – the mission statement – it should be as clear and concise as possible. People should be able to remember it and communicate it to others.

On a personal level, your mission is the red line through your (working) life, the element, that fulfills you, that makes you happy, that helps you make (career) decisions.

Mission and culture are strongly related to each other, because culture means, ideally, living the mission as a team, as an organization. The problem is: In every team, in every organization, culture is being formed from the first day on. Over time culture emerges, it cannot be planed or set up or adopted in a single day.

In his Organizational Culture Model, Edgar Schein, a renowned former Professor at MIT Sloane School of Management, identified three levels of organizational culture, and compared them to an iceberg: At the top, visible for everyone, are the artifacts and behaviors – everything that can be viewed, heard, felt, from the way people dress to the way they interact with each other and the outside world. Below are the "espoused" values, for example rules, codes, principles, policies and – strategies. Going down deeper, below the water, are the basic assumptions, the granted beliefs, deeply embedded in an organization and hard to recognize. Though they are usually unconscious, they constitute the essence of culture. According to Schein, organizational culture is "the primary source of resistance to change".

Therefore, cultural understanding is essential for leaders and entrepreneurs as part of their strategic thinking. And, it is not only important to understand your own culture, but also the culture of your clients, your stakeholders and other players you want to have an impact on. There is a clear interdependency between culture and strategy. Strategy is part of the culture, and culture has an influence on strategy. If a new strategy does not conform with the culture, it will not work.

⊠ [8] THE THREE LEVELS OF CULTURE ACCORDING TO EDGAR SCHEIN

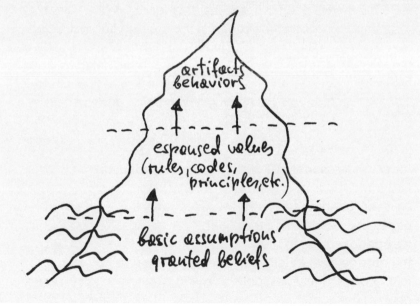

TOOL

| 5 |

THE SQUARE TRIANGLE

Source: Frank Boos, Gerald Mitterer

PHASE

Analyzing and implementing.

TOPIC

Analyze and understand your culture. Consider the relationship between strategy & organizational structure & the people in the organization when implementing new strategies.

HOW TO APPLY

From a systemic point of view, the three columns of an organization or business are: the strategy, the organizational structure, the people and their behavior. In the middle, influenced by the three columns, is the culture. Describe your three columns, how they look, how they are manifested. Then describe the culture. This analysis helps you to find the triggering point for change, for focusing and acting. Development should always be along a balanced triangle. When it's out of balance, you need to adapt accordingly.

TIP

Organizational development means personal development as
well. Designing change is always working on one's own identity,
too. In a time, where the need for change is constantly rising,
where change follows change, working on one's own identity
and culture becomes a permanent activity.

⊠ [9] THE SQUARE TRIANGLE AS A MODEL FOR ORGANIZATIONAL DEVELOPMENT

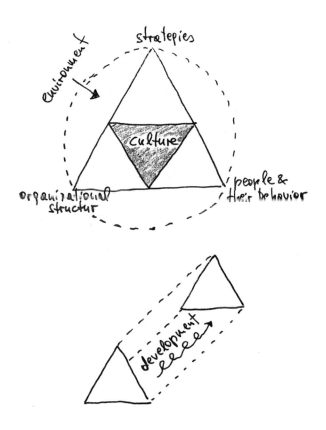

TOOL

6

THE PATH OF LIFE

Source: Beratergruppe Neuwaldegg

PHASE

Analyzing

TOPIC

Contemplating the future is only possible when taking the past into consideration. Why? Because in the past, all your knowledge, experience and competences, as well as your patterns and culture, were formed. For developing strategies, you need to decide what to leave behind and what to take with you.

HOW TO APPLY

Draw your path of life or that of your organization, your business: Where and when did you / it start? What were the major milestones and projects? What were points of change when the journey took a different direction, or when a dramatic event forced you to change? While remembering and recalling your journey, your drawing will unfold.

Analyzing the drawing, you can find out a lot about yourself and your organization. What did you collect on the way? All your experience, knowledge, know-how, values, attitudes, patterns, failures should be considered. What phases did you go through? What triggered change? To what internal and external challenges and circumstances did you react and in what way? Where do you stand now?

COMMENT

The Path of Life Model is based on the systemic concept of
self-organization: Any organization is a social system, an entity,
whose essential communicative activities consist of a sequence
of linked decisions. As such, it follows an evolutionary path,
guided by patterns, that are specific to the individual organization. These patterns form the modus operandi, the flow of
communication and the process of decision-making. You cannot
change the system itself, but you can influence it by impulses
and interventions, that are accepted and become effective.

⊠ [10] PATH OF LIFE

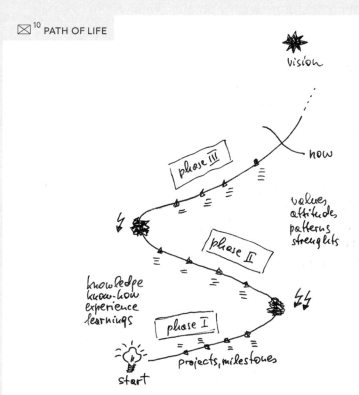

TOOL

7

DIAMOND OF VALUES

Source: Roswita Königswieser

PHASE

Anytime

TOPIC

Our behavior is driven by our values and attitudes, by what we believe is important in our work and in our life. Values result in how we view the world, how we communicate, interact and decide. Therefore, we should be aware and clear about them.

HOW TO APPLY

Think about your values and how they affect your work, your business. Choose 5–7 most precious and effective values, you want to stand for in the future, that should guide you and be the basis of all your activities, decisions and the way you com-municate. Visualize them in the form of a diamond, as if it were a gift to yourself and everyone around. If you work as a team, you should come up with those values, that you all agree to and make that the basis for your teamwork.

⊠ ¹¹ DIAMOND OF VALUES

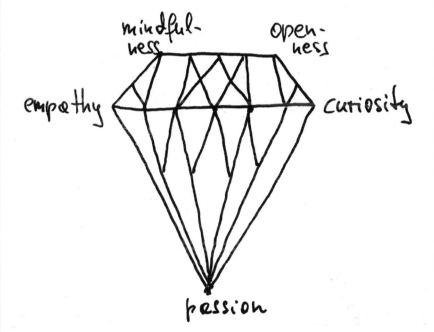

Core Competencies

Building your strategies on your resources and abilities is an advice for entrepreneurs who aim at creating impact over mere profit, who think and act in networks and co-operations rather than competition and who highly identify with what they are doing. Building your strategies on your resources and abilities means building your strategies on your core competencies. But what are core competencies?

The concept of core competencies as a strategic tool was first introduced in 1990 by business academics Gary Hamel and Coimbatore Prahalad, as an approach for organizations, who, instead of fighting off the competition, wanted to create and move into new markets. For Hamel and Prahalad, core competencies are the collective learning in an organization, a combination of specific, collaborative, integrated and applied knowledge, skills and attitude. A combination, that is unique – the single competencies might not be unique, but the "bundle" is – and cannot be imitated by others.

In our context, core competencies constitute the essence of what a business is, the main source of potential even in rapidly changing times. Core competencies include your values and attitudes, your skills, your strengths, your know-how and knowledge, a specific technological resource, a specific space, even your network and access to a specific community.

TOOL

8

QUESTIONNAIRE

Source: My adaption based on Hamel / Prahalad, Reinhard Nagel

PHASE

Analyzing

TOPIC

Identifying your core competencies as the roots of your business and as the basis for your strategies.

HOW TO APPLY

The questionnaire helps you to identify your core competencies by collecting all your knowledge, skills and attitudes, seen from different aspects and perspectives. First you collect, then you combine. Only the combination results in core competencies that are decisive for your success. It is, again, an experimental approach, like putting together a puzzle.

INTERNAL ANALYSIS
° Knowledge and know-how
° Values and attitudes
° Culture and style
° Resources
° Experience and learnings
° Strength and social skills

SUCCESS STORIES OF THE PAST

◦ What were the most successful projects / products?
◦ What determined the success?
◦ What projects, solutions and stories am I / are we especially
  proud of?
◦ What is the red line through my / our path of life in business?

EXTERNAL ANALYSIS

◦ What do my / our clients and beneficiaries say about me / us?
◦ What benefits and impact do I / we have on them?
◦ What is the significant difference to the benefits and impact
  of comparable products / services / solutions on the market?
◦ What do my / our colleagues and stakeholders say about
  me / us?
◦ What do they value about me / us?
◦ If I / we think of outsourcing, what could not be done by others?
◦ For whom am I / are we a benchmark and why?

Impact Modeling

Along with the rise of social entrepreneurship, that aims at solving the most pressing problems society is facing today with an entrepreneurial spirit, new tools and methods for impact-oriented business modeling and reporting have been created. They, in my opinion, not only work in the field of social entrepreneurship, but help in general to turn ideas into change-making strategies, shifting yours and your client's perspective.

The main difference to traditional business modeling in the 20th century is the impact-orientation instead of mere profit-orientation. Impact is defined as a social change as consequence of your activities. The starting point is a social problem and its causes that you want to address. Your vision is a future without the specific problem. Therefore, the business model does not aim at producing an output, but an outcome. Output is the work performed, whereas outcome goes a step further and is defined as the results achieved by virtue of the output. Output and outcome can have different dimensions (SEE ILL. 12 RESULT LADDER), with for example, changes in society, changes in paradigms and system change, at the highest level.

⊠ [12] RESULT LADDER (Source: SRS, Phineo gAG)

7 society changes

6 target groups life situation changes

5 target groups change their behavior

4 target groups change their skills

Outcome & Impact
→ results

3 target groups accept offer

2 target groups are reached

1 activities occur as planned

Output
→ work performed

TOOL

IMPACT MODEL

Source: Social Reporting Standard (SRS)

PHASE

Analyzing and Creating.

TOPIC

The impact value chain of a business model.

HOW TO APPLY

Describe and define your impact model by going through the single steps as outlined in the impact matrix ^(SEE ILL. 13 IMPACT MATRIX) and answering the questions below.

THE SOCIAL PROBLEM
- Which specific social problem should be solved?
- Why is it a problem, what are the root causes and consequences of the problem?
- How big ist the problem? How will the situation develop in the future, if nothing is done?
- Who is affected by the problem?
- What are the related costs of the problem for society and who bears these costs?

THE VISION

° Describe the vision that your offer or offers have been designed to realize!
° What ideal societal situation are you striving for?
° How does the world look 5–20 years from now, when you are successful?
° What are the related costs of the problem for society and who bears these costs?
° Who is affected by the problem?
° What are your long-term goals? (5–20 years)

YOUR APPROACH

° What are the main activities you take to achieve an impact? What is your solution?
° Describe where you will implement your activities in the value chain, and what you will offer the target group, as well as what results and changes you expect to see.
° Describe the narrative and the theoretical background of your approach, behind your activities and offers.

TARGET GROUPS

° What are the main activities you take to achieve an impact? What is your solution?
° Describe where you will implement your activities in the value chain, and what you will offer the target group, as well as what results and changes you expect to see.
° Describe the narrative and the theoretical background of your approach, behind your activities and offers.

INPUT

All the resources you need to produce and deliver your offer:
◦ Financial resources: personnel and operating costs, including
  administrative costs What is your solution?
◦ Material resources: property, rooms, equipment, facilities
◦ Time resources: hours contributed by you, by the staff and
  by pro-bono partners

OUTPUT

All the work performed, the products and services which result
from your activities:
◦ Short description of your products, services and work
  performed

OUTCOME
◦ What changes should occur in the direct and / or indirect target
  groups as a direct result of your work?
◦ How can you obtain and record the achieved results? Can they
  be measured and if so, which indicators can be considered?
◦ What alternative or supplementary information and activities
  can support your offer? (expert assessments, recommendations,
  etc.)?

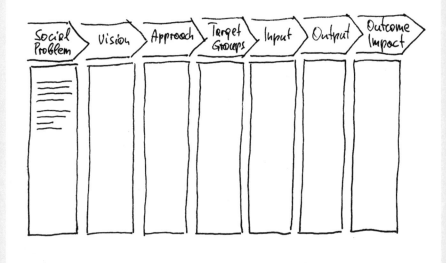

⊠ 13 IMPACT MATRIX

Market and Ecosystem

To know your clients, your stakeholders and everyone else in your business ecosystem is crucial for developing strategies, even if you follow a resource-based view, driven by your vision, mission, core competencies and passion. Your environment is constantly changing, so as part of your strategic thinking you should pay attention to everything around you with careful attention to be able to identify opportunities and act proactively.

The traditional concept, that the market is dominated by competitors, is massively changing. Co-operations, networks, hubs, open source and other forms of collaborative practices are the future, particularly for entrepreneurs. Developing a cooperative attitude, a sense of empathy and mindfulness towards your environment is therefore helpful.

YOU SHOULD IDENTIFY
- Who are the relevant players in and for your business, from colleagues to suppliers to clients to stakeholders to network partners?
- What are their needs, expectations and potential?
- What cultural, ethical and other rules, codes, dynamics and restrictions are influencing their behavior and decisions?
- What future trends and drivers of change are emerging?
- What is the bigger picture and context, what are the most pressing challenges economy and society are facing?

From the following tools, a couple are service design tools. Service design is a relatively new approach in design, aiming to improve the quality and interaction between a provider and a customer. It's a human centered, systemic approach focusing on the experience of a service, providing tools, that are useful not only in the design context.

TOOL

10

STAKEHOLDER ANALYSIS

Source: project management tradition

PHASE

Analyzing

TOPIC

Analyze your environment and your relationships: Who has an influence on your business, who needs to be involved and how?

HOW TO APPLY

As a first step, you brainstorm and make a list of who are the external environments and stakeholders, that are involved in or affected by your business, from target groups to suppliers to potential partners to influential communities. Then you evaluate them according to the following parameters:
° Intensity of contact (1 high intensity, 2 average, 3 low)
° Influence on your success (1 high influence, 2 average, 3 low)

In the next step you draw a map, where you arrange the stakeholders in concentric circles around you. A high intensity contact is in the inner circle, a low one in the outer circle. The influence is represented by a symbol of your own choice, for example an asterisk for high influence, a small dot for low influence.

The resulting map gives you a clear picture about your relationships to the outside world and how to improve them, meet their needs as well as benefit from them. If an important stakeholder is in the outer circle, what can you do to bring him closer to you? You can also compare the status quo with future scenarios – who is important now, who will be important in the future?

TIP

Particularly in the field of social entrepreneurship, major social challenges are too big and complex to be solved individually or by one sector of people. There is a need for a collective impact. How, as businesses, can we work together, how can we learn from each other, how can we build alliances, how can our networks become strong movements? Interpret your stakeholder analysis as an ecosystem, that can support your change-making strategies.

⊠ ¹⁴ STAKEHOLDER ANALYSIS

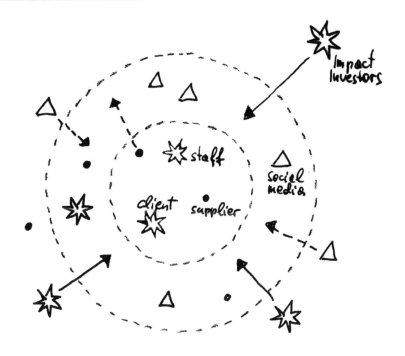

☆ high
△ average
• low

INFLUENCE

INTENSITY OF
CONTACT

TOOL

11

CUSTOMER SATISFACTION

Source: Reinhart Nagel; marketing tradition

PHASE

Analyzing (for existing businesses and their customers)

TOPIC

Analyzing your clients and customers' satisfaction by evaluating your output.

HOW TO APPLY

First you identify a list of relevant criteria that are important for your clients or customers satisfaction. Then you rate them, taking your customers point of view. A low rate indicates a weakness in your performance, a high rate a strength. Analyzing the strengths and weaknesses you can derive strategies for improvement.

You can do this analysis for every one of your clients, if your services and their needs are different with each client. Otherwise you can work out a general analysis.

> TIP
> To get an authentic view you can also conduct interviews with your clients and customers.

⊠ 15 CUSTOMER SATISFACTION MATRIX

criteria for satisfaction	rating 1 2 3 4 5	streughts	weakness

what can we do to improve?

— —
— —
— —

TOOL

12

PERSONAS & STORYWORLDS

Source: service design

PHASE

Analyzing

TOPIC

To know clearly the demands, needs, desires and living conditions of your clients, customers and beneficiaries to ensure your work is relevant for them.

HOW TO APPLY

A persona is a fictional character that represents a group / segment / community of potential customers and users of your product or service. Personas are created by drawing together the characteristics of similar people into one archetype through which the group can be understood.

Even if a persona is fictional, their profile should be based on research, interviews and observations. Personas are usually described by: name / age / other demographic information / looks / education / profession and working context / lifestyle and living condition / interests, skills, etc.

A storyworld goes even more into details. It is a worksheet about a personas world, creating a whole story about their context and self-perception. Who is this person connected to and how? What physical and digital objects and places is this person connected to? What does this person think or believe about themselves and the world around them? What shapes their values and attitudes, what drives their visions?

TIP

Make your personas and storyworlds visually striking by adding photos and other illustration material that you collect from magazines, reports, etc.

⊠ 16 PERSONAS & STORYWORLDS

TOOL

13

DRIVERS OF CHANGE

Source: service design

PHASE

Analyzing

TOPIC

New types of questions are being asked by markets, by stake-holders, by the environment, by society – the underlying impulses are acting as drivers of change. These drivers become more and more powerful and effective, plus news ones emerge and add to the complexity. A fact, that forces us more than ever to analyze the outside world and integrate this analysis into our strategies and our development as a constant process.

HOW TO APPLY

Brainstorm and collect topics and movements, that act as drivers of change. Collect as many as possible, as diverse as possible, and even think about the far future. As a help, you can take the so-called STEEP-categories as a reference, based on their main area of impact: Societal, Technological, Economic, Environmental, and Political. Draw a diagram and post all your collected topics along the two axis of uncertainty and influence on your business [SEE ILL. 17] and analyze the result.

TIP

There are institutions and agencies, that offer sets of cards with hundreds of drivers they've identified, providing them as workshop material and a helpful tool in this exercise.

☒ [17] DRIVERS OF CHANGE

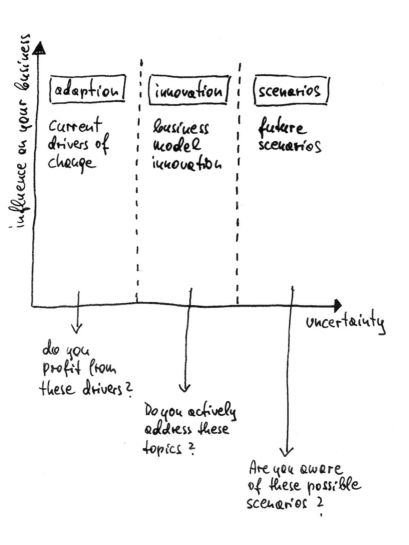

TODA

Innovation and Scaling

Analyzing yourself and your environment provides you with all the information, insights and assumptions you need to create strategies – that is developing a road map for the future: Where do you want to go with your business, what direction, and what are the different options along the way?

As we said before, this is an experimental and creative approach. You mix and match the internal and external factors and parameters that you analyzed so far, you synthesize the past with the future, your vision and your core competencies with opportunities in the market.

Depending on the need and your capability for change you might go for adaptive or innovative strategies:

- Based on your existing business model, you might strengthen your position within your existing target group and ecosystem.
- Based on your existing business model, you might expand into new markets.
- You might innovate your business model within your existing target group and ecosystem.
- You might innovate your business model and open new markets with it.

From small steps to major moves, from improving your communication to developing new services or products your strategic direction should be based on what feels right for you. There is no objective right or wrong, only your entrepreneurial spirit and the will to change.

In the context of social businesses, the strategy of scaling – that is growing your impact and increasing the number of people reached – is crucial for a successful social innovation. Scalable innovations are relevant beyond their initial context by not relying on the talent of a specific person but on the power of the ecosystem.

TOOL

| 14 |

CORE COMPETENCE MATRIX

Source: Gary Hamel and C.K. Prahalad

PHASE

Creating and developing strategies.

TOPIC

Developing market growth strategies by using your core competences.

HOW TO APPLY

Take the core competencies matrix [(SEE ILL. 18)] as a tool to develop scenarios and options, according to the four areas of:

FILLING IN THE BLANKS
What core competencies can be used in existing markets to improve your services and thus strengthen your position?

PREMIER PLUS TEN
Imagine in ten years time, what new core competencies will you have developed to maintain and strengthen your position?

WHITE SPACES
White spaces are chances or opportunities, you have not seen so far. What core competencies co from new opportunities and expand into new markets?

MEGA OPPORTUNITIES
What new core competencies could you develop, to expand into new markets?

⊠ [18] CORE COMPETENCE MATRIX

	existing core competencies	new core competencies
existing markets	filling in the blanks	premier plus ten
new markets	white spaces	mega opportunities

TOOL

15

SWOT ANALYSIS

Source: Albert S. Humphrey

PHASE

Analyzing and developing.

TOPIC

One of the most common tools to generate strategic options based on the combination of internal strengths and weaknesses with external opportunities and threats.

HOW TO APPLY

Completing a SWOT analysis involves identifying and mapping the internal and external factors that are assisting or hindering you in achieving your goal. First you collect those strengths and weaknesses in you or your organization as well as the opportunities and threads you see in the market. Some of these factors you might have already identified by using other analyzing tools. Having completed each of the quadrants in the worksheet matrix (SEE ILL. 19), you can now draw your conclusions and develop scenarios by combining the four SWOT-factors. This last step of the exercise is sometimes called TOWS-Analysis. It delivers the true value of the tool by using the results to maximize the positive influences on your business and minimize the negative ones.

⊠ [19] SWOT-MATRIX

	internal strenghts	internal weaknesses
market opportunities	SO-strategies	WO-strategies
market threats	ST-strategies	WT-strategies

SO-STRATEGIES

What opportunities match your strengths and how can you use this match strategically?

WO-STRATEGIES

Are there any opportunities that can turn your weaknesses into strengths? What activities can you take to minimize your weaknesses regarding opportunities?

ST-STRATEGIES

What strengths will help you prevent or minimize threats from outside?

WT-STRATEGIES

What can you do so your weaknesses don't threaten your future, how can you minimize them, especially in the context of external threats?

TIP

The SWOT analysis provides a good framework for reviewing current strategies and directions, or test new ideas and projects. Therefore, you should have a specific question / topic / project that you want to address, when using this tool.

TOOL

16

BUSINESS MODEL INNOVATION

Source: innovation management

PHASE

Creating and developing strategies.

TOPIC

A business model innovation is the conscious change of an existing business model as a framework of how to approach innovation that is not based on a technological innovation.

HOW TO APPLY

A business model innovation views innovations as changes to the three main aspects or decisions, that make up a business model: WHAT are you offering for WHOM and HOW. It's not about a technological innovation. It's about combining existing products or services with existing markets and existing technologies in a new mix or a special focus. The innovation lies in the new combination of existing ideas. You could, for example, combine one aspect of your existing business model with an aspect of a business model from a different industry or sector. This is what Apple did with iTunes, by looking at the music industry. You can also aim at a systemic change, by changing the fundamental paradigms of an existing business model. Changes in customer behaviors and values are supporting such innovations. This is what the whole sharing economy is about. Social innovation is also aiming at systemic changes. Therefore, business model innovations have the potential to revolutionize an entire industry or sector.

To approach business model innovation, you start with your own or an existing model and experiment by mixing and matching ideas of new combinations. This might need additional research: How do other business models work, in other industries or sectors? On what changes are other business model innovations based on? What are the market dynamics and value chains, the public policy and industry norms, the cultural implications? For visualizing your ideas, you can use the business model introduced in this book (SEE PAGE 81 / TOOL 1) or the business model canvas developed by Alexander Osterwalder, which is more elaborate.

✉ 20 BUSINESS MODEL INNOVATION

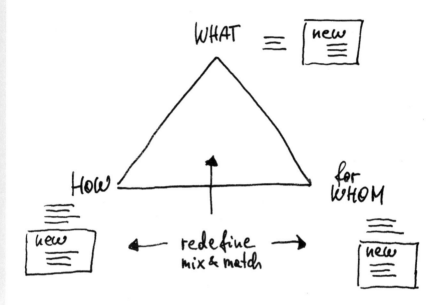

TOOL

17

TRANSFER & SCALING MODELS

Source: Ashoka

PHASE

Creating and developing strategies for existing social businesses and programs.

TOPIC

Creating strategies for social businesses that grow your impact and increase the number of people reached.

HOW TO APPLY

The key question in creating scaling strategies are WHAT to transfer, WHERE to transfer, HOW to transfer and WHO to address as a transfer partner.

WHAT TO TRANSFER

What is it that you want to transfer? Is it your whole business, your organization, is it a program (activities) or is it principles and approaches (e.g. guidelines about how to serve a particular social purpose)? This is about defining your core components that are transferable.

WHERE TO TRANSFER

This is about identifying the kind and scope of your transfer partners (is it an individual entrepreneur or organization or is it a group, community or network) as well as the appropriate geography. For this you may define some criteria like where is the problem most pressing, where is it most aligned with our general strategy, where is it most efficient, where is the best funding and business opportunity, etc.

HOW TO TRANSFER

The basic transfer models are growth, affiliation and dissemination. Growth means growing within the original organization, by expanding, by mergers and acquisitions. Affiliation is when an ongoing relationship with an implementing partner is formed, generally within a legal framework that sets out the nature of relationship. This can be licensing, franchising, joint venture, etc. Dissemination is about sharing or exchanging information and best practice openly with others. It's mostly an informal and loosely structured relationship, like open sourcing, training, consulting and smart networks. Growth is about direct impact and more control. Dissemination is about indirect impact, less control, and more openness. The option will depend on how much you want to be actively involved, what your resources are, what kind of skills and expertise is needed, and how fast you want to spread your impact.

WHO TO ADDRESS

Which type of partners are you looking for: funders, implementers, networkers, etc.? Partner profiles help you to define the key characteristics and roles they should fulfill, from synergies to culture to strategies. These should fit with the key requirements needed for a successful replication.

Conclusion and Outlook

I hope I have shown you how, as a creative and social entrepreneur, you can create your own sustainable future as well as contribute to a sustainable environment. Much remains to be said. As an ongoing process, strategic thinking is lifelong learning. Tools and methods can help you approach this ongoing process. The way you perceive yourself and everything around you is a key to this process. Implementing your strategies is still another story. It means planning – your activities, your resources, your time frame and schedule.

To implement strategies, you need to think about the organizational structure for its execution, the operational processes and the people involved. You need to think about communication and storytelling, about how you want to spread your mission, what kind of story you want to tell and how. Like the process itself, this is an ongoing list of topics. They might result in another book …

the CENTRE FOR SOCIAL I
COWORKING
community & LA
for people who are
the world jo

get workspace

References

BERATERGRUPPE NEUWALDEGG:
Strategie: Jazz oder Symphonie? Aktuelle Beispiele strategischer
Improvisation, Wien 1995.

BOOS, FRANK / MITTERER, GERALD:
Einführung in das systemische Management, Heidelberg 2014.

DRUCKER, PETER:
Innovation and Entrepreneurship, New York 1999.

DRUCKER, PETER:
The Essential Drucker, New York, 2001.

ESCHENBACH, ROLF / ESCHENBACH,
SEBASTIAN / KUNESCH, HERBERT:
Strategische Konzepte. Management-Ansätze von Ansoff bis
Ulrich, 4. Aufl., Stuttgart 2003.

HAMEL, GARY / PRAHALAD, C.K.:
The Core Competence of the Corporation,
in: Harvard Business Review, May–June 1990.

PRAHALAD, C. K. & HAMEL, G.:
Strategy as a field of study: Why search for a new paradigm?
In: Strategic management journal, 15 / 1994, 5–16.

KÖNIGSWIESER, ROSWITA / EXNER, ALEXANDER:
Systemische Intervention. Architekturen und Designs für Berater
und Veränderungsmanager, 9. Aufl., Stuttgart 2006.

MINTZBERG, HENRY:
Crafting Strategy, in: Harvard Business Review, July 1987
(Online-Version).

MINTZBERG, HENRY:
Strategic Thinking as Seeing, in: B. Garratt (Hrsg.), Developing
Strategic Thought, S. 67–70, London 1995.

MINTZBERG, HENRY / AHLSTRAND, BRUCE / LAMPEL,
JOSEPH:
Strategy Safari. A Guided Tour Through The Wilds Of Strategic
Management, New York 1998.

NAGEL, REINHART:
Lust auf Strategie. Workbook zur systemischen Strategie-
entwicklung, 2. Aufl., Stuttgart 2009.

ORGANISATIONSENTWICKLUNG – ZEITSCHRIFT
FÜR UNTERNEHMENSENTWICKLUNG UND CHANGE
MANAGEMENT, Online-Ausgabe 4 / 2007.

PORTER, MICHAEL E.: What is strategy? In: Harvard Business
Review, November / December 1996 (Online-Version).

SCHEIN, EDGAR H.: Organizational Culture and Leadership,
5th Edition, Hoboken, New Jersey 2017.

Imprint

Doris Rothauer, Vienna and New York
www.dorisrothauer.com

TRANSLATION:
Doris Rothauer

COPY-EDITING:
Ed Neumeister

GRAPHIC DESIGN:
brand unit, Vienna
www.brand-unit.com

PHOTOS:
All © Doris Rothauer
Except Studio Sagmeister & Walsh (pages 44–45, 67),
© Sagmeister & Walsh

Photos were shot at the following sites and studios:
Centre for Social Innovation, New York
Franklyn Design Studio, New York
Impact Hub, New York
Sagmeister & Walsh, New York
TODA Design Firm, New York

ILLUSTRATIONS:
All © Doris Rothauer

Except:
III. 1: MOTMOT Design
III. 3: Bend the Rules, designed by Arash and Kelly

Library of Congress Cataloging-in-Publication data
A CIP catalog record for this book has been applied for
at the Library of Congress.

Bibliographic information published by the German
National Library
The German National Library lists this publication in the
Deutsche Nationalbibliografie; detailed bibliographic data
are available on the Internet at http://dnb.dnb.de.

Printed on acid-free and chlorine-free bleached paper,
FSC certified.

PRINTED IN AUSTRIA

ISBN 978-3-0356-1492-3

This publication is also available as an e-book
(ISBN PDF 978-3-0356-1496-1)
© 2018 Birkhäuser Verlag GmbH, Basel P.O. Box 44,
4009 Basel, Switzerland
Part of Walter de Gruyter GmbH, Berlin / Boston

DORIS ROTHAUER

Doris Rothauer is a consultant, coach, expert and author connecting the creative, economic and social worlds. It's her mission to promote creativity as the key to a new economy and society based on a paradigm shift and a more holistic view.

As a strategy consultant and coach, she helps entrepreneurs from the creative industries and social businesses as well as artists and art institutions to manage their creativity and turn their visions into successful strategies.

She holds a PhD in Economics from the Vienna University of Economics and Business, a Masters Degree in art management and a professional training certificate as a systemic coach and consultant. She is also an alumni of the Ashoka Visionary Program by Ashoka Austria.

After 15 years of working as an art manager in the art world, including leading positions in major art institutions, such as Director of the Vienna Secession and the Künstlerhaus Wien, she founded her own company, Büro für Transfer, in 2006. Since then she has been working with more than 80 artists, entrepreneurs, companies and institutions building up an impressive network of clients and partners.